MANAGING YOUR
MONEY AND FINANCES™

Managing
Finances
and Shopping
Online

Xina M. Uhl and Judy Monroe Peterson

Rosen
YA™
New York

Published in 2020 by The Rosen Publishing Group, Inc.
29 East 21st Street, New York, NY 10010

Library of Congress Cataloging-in-Publication Data

Names: Uhl, Xina M., author. | Peterson, Judy Monroe, author.
Title: Managing finances and shopping online /
Xina M. Uhl and Judy Monroe Peterson.
Description: First edition. | New York : Rosen Publishing,
2020. | Series: Managing your money and finances |
Includes bibliographical references and index.
Identifiers: LCCN 2018048117| ISBN 9781508188407
(library bound) | ISBN 9781508188391 (pbk.)
Subjects: LCSH: Internet banking—Juvenile literature.
| Electronic commerce—Juvenile literature. | Electronic
funds transfers—Juvenile literature. | Finance, Personal—
Juvenile. | Consumer education—Juvenile literature.
Classification: LCC HG1710 .U45 2020 |
DDC 332.02400285/4678—dc23
LC record available at https://lccn.loc.gov/2018048117

Manufactured in the United States of America

CONTENTS

INTRODUCTION

Among the many wonders of the computer age is the ability to perform everyday tasks online in a quick and easy way. Having access to banking information on the internet through websites and apps makes it easier to keep track of expenses, transfer money, and pay bills. Credit cards, debit cards, and other forms of payment such as PayPal, Venmo, and Zelle have both benefits and dangers that should be considered.

More advanced financial transactions like investments can also be completed without leaving the house. This convenience can be especially helpful for people who live in remote areas or who have health problems that keep them homebound.

An explosion of online storefronts have opened along with the development of technology. Sometimes these put physical, or brick-and-mortar, stores out of business due to increased competition. While certain online retailers are well known, such as Amazon and eBay, a number of others exist, too. In order to use these sites safely

Credit cards allow for instant purchases on computers, tablets, and smartphones. Visa, MasterCard, and Discover cards are all-purpose and accepted at most online stores.

and obtain the best deals possible, it is necessary to learn how to check reviews about these sites. Comparison shopping helps teens get the most from their money. The step-by-step directions in this guide help teens to become familiar with how to conduct shopping, seek out reviews, and compare deals. The latest smartphone apps that make these activities easy are covered. So are special deals like social coupons and other promotional deals.

Some online stores, like eBay, operate as auction houses. The advantage of using online auction houses are many. They include the ability to find used, obscure items. Buyers can also get better prices than at stores with fixed prices because they may or may not be competing against other buyers who want the same item. The ins and outs of these online auctions are also explored.

While online shopping can be fun and practical, teens should keep their budget in mind. By deciding in advance what they really need and what they can afford, teens can avoid financial problems and make wise buying decisions. A number of high-tech and low-tech strategies help to keep budgets in check. Shopping online has definite advantages. But there are costs as well. These include shipping and handling fees.

Along with the speed and convenience of online banking and shopping come a number of dangers. These include scams and fraud. Individuals' private information such as credit card numbers, Social Security numbers, and passwords are at risk from online thieves. Identity theft is an ever-present danger in today's world. It is necessary for teens to protect their information as much as possible to keep from dealing with identity theft and fraud.

As online shopping and financial management become more complex, it is necessary to keep up with the changing times. By learning smart, safe practices early in life, teens can face the future more confident in their abilities to handle their money and their purchases.

CHAPTER ONE

Banking and Paying Bills Online

Managing money and staying within a budget is fast and easy with online tools, smartphone apps, and financial software. While some people may feel more comfortable entering purchases into a spreadsheet, others use mobile banking and financial apps instead.

Internet Banking Services

Virtual (online) banks and most brick-and-mortar banks offer online services. The Federal Reserve System, the Federal Deposit Insurance Corporation (FDIC), and federal banking agencies regulate both types of banks. Virtual banks provide many of the same services as regular banks. However, people cannot walk in and do face-to-face transactions with tellers or bankers. People can go in person to physical banks. Wells Fargo, Bank of America, Citibank, US Bank, and other large banks have branch offices

Shopping online means you cannot pay cash for your purchases. Credit cards and debit cards are crucial.

across the country. Local community banks are also widely available.

Most virtual and regular banks post a lot of information on their websites about their accounts and services. Using a computer or smartphone, teens can research and compare the services of different banks and credit unions. Credit unions are non-profit financial institutions owned by the people who use them. Like banks, they are regulated by the federal government.

Banks and credit unions offer many kinds of accounts, including checking accounts. They usually charge fees for their different checking accounts and other financial services. Basic or low-activity accounts often require people to pay a small monthly fee and maintain a minimum balance. Free checking accounts are sometimes available, but they usually do not pay interest and they may have fees for certain services.

Some banks require teens to open an online joint checking account with a cosigner, such as a parent or guardian. If a problem occurs with the account, the cosigner will assume responsibility. Other banks have special checking accounts for students. Teens usually do not pay a monthly fee, but they may have some limitations in using the account.

Typical Online Features

Many people find online banking to be a useful tool for following their budget and tracking money. They can access their account at any time, and they do not need to fill out paper forms to do money transactions. Once they log in to their account, people can check the balance, transfer money between

Banks like Chase, Bank of America, and others are national institutions while credit unions are local.

accounts, view statements, and pay bills. Account information can be downloaded to personal-finance software like Quicken or AceMoney, or popular apps like Mint, Acorn, or YNAB.

To use a bank's online features, customers fill out an application and choose a username, password, and personal identification number (PIN). They also sign an official signature authorization form. The bank keeps customers' signatures on file to prevent fraud. Finally, people make a deposit to open the account. They can now go to the bank's site and log in with their username or number and password. Every site differs, but online banking information usually looks like printed bank statements. It shows deposits (money added) and withdrawals (money taken out) of an account. On many sites, clicking a link next to a check number displays a picture of the canceled check.

Choose a PIN that thieves cannot easily figure out. A PIN should never include the year you were born, your Social Security number, or your phone number.

While most people pay for purchases with debit or credit cards, some people use personal checks. Most merchants process checks electronically. In a store, paper checks are run through an electronic system that sends information from the check (not the check itself) to a bank or other financial institution. The funds are then transferred into the store's account. Customers get a copy of the signed receipt. for their records. They also get their check back, which is marked and cannot be used again. Similarly, many companies and individuals now digitally send information on checks to banks to transfer funds into their accounts. An overdraft penalty is charged if not enough money is in the account to cover a check.

Transferring Money

With online banking, people can move money instantly between accounts at the same bank. Teens might deposit their paycheck into a checking account and then transfer some of it into their savings account to earn interest. Then they can move money from savings to checking when making payments for things they need, such as car repairs. Most banks handle transfers on the same business day, or the next day if the transfer occurs after a cutoff time. For example, some banks process transfers on the same day if they are made before 3:00 p.m.

Many banks allow people to make electronic transfers to and from accounts at other banks. However, the transferred money may take two to seven days to show up. Most banks charge a fee for transfers between banks.

Paying Bills

Most banks and credit unions provide online bill paying. This service is often free and can save people money because they do not need to buy checks, stamps, and envelopes. Instead, they go online and authorize the bank to transfer money from their account to pay bills. People can use this method for one-time payments or recurring payments (for example, payments that occur once every month). Using online bill paying can help give people peace of mind and better management of what gets paid and when.

Google Wallet is a handy app when it comes to sending or receiving money from a smartphone or other device.

To set up electronic bill payment service, people log in to their checking account and go to Bill Pay or something similar. They choose the companies to pay. If a company is not listed, customers can enter the account number and the name and address. Then, whenever they need to, they can go to their bank account, choose a company, and enter the amount to pay and the date. The bank moves the money out of the account and transfers it to the company on the specified date.

Many people like the convenience of their bank's automatic bill paying service for routine monthly bills. They use it to pay their rent, auto and insurance payments, cell phone bills, and more. Many banks offer this service for free, but others charge a fee. Using automatic bill paying ensures that bills are paid on time and for the correct amount. This feature can save people time and worry about paying their bills on time. To set up the service, people tell the bank which bills they want to pay automatically. Then the bank takes money from their checking account to pay the same amount monthly on a specified day of the month.

PayPal, Zelle, and Venmo are other methods of paying bills or sending money to friends or family. Each of these apps requires customers to sign up for an account and link that account to their checking account, debit card, or credit card. PayPal requires the email of the person to be paid. Zelle and Venmo require either the phone number or email address of the person or business to be paid. The advantage of using these apps is that they transfer money quickly and easily.

Keeping an Eye on Your Finances

People may run into problems when paying bills online. For example, they might continue to make automatic payments for products and services they no longer want or need. Forgetting

The Mechanics of Money Transfers

Most online money transfers are processed through the Automated Clearing House (ACH) network. This electronic-funds transfer system uses computer technology instead of paper checks and forms. ACH is used for payroll direct deposits; e-checks; credit cards and debit cards; payments for rent, loans, and insurance premiums; and federal and state tax payments. When a bank sends payment for a bill, the company receives an ACH transfer or a paper check. ACH transfers are fast and reliable, although not all companies use this feature. The company usually receives the payments the next day, and the funds are moved almost instantly. Paper checks issued by a bank are mailed through the US Postal Service and take longer to arrive.

about the payments or finding it easier to do nothing, they continue to get charged. Teens should review their bills every month and decide whether their ongoing payments fit their budget. Another reason to check online bills and accounts regularly is to watch for errors and report them to the bank right away. When people switch checking accounts, they need to reset their automated bill payments. People must also update their automatic payment information if a credit card account expires or is closed and reopened with a new number.

Young people can avoid unpleasant surprises in the form of overdraft fees if they keep a minimum balance in their checking accounts.

If teens spend more money than they have in their account, the bank issues an overdraft notice and charges a fee. This fee can be costly because the bank charges for each check or transaction that cannot be paid. The bank also returns the electronic or paper check to the company, which often adds its own fee. To avoid piling up these penalty costs, teens can keep extra money in their checking account. They also need to remember to subtract the amount for each paid bill from their account balance. Some banks offer automatic email reminders when bills are due. People can also use their computers or smartphones to create automatic reminders.

Another way to avoid extra fees is to sign up for overdraft protection. This electronic service links a person's checking and savings accounts. If not enough money is in the checking account to pay a bill, the funds are pulled from the linked savings account.

CHAPTER TWO

Credit Cards, Debit Cards, and More

Banks have a number of special features that make managing money convenient and effortless. These features may come with a cost, though, so it is important to keep track of how much money is deposited and how much is removed.

Borrowing on Credit

Banks and other financial institutions issue credit cards. These plastic cards allow people to borrow money for buying clothing, gas, movies, music, concert tickets, and many other things. Credit is a temporary loan, and the money must be repaid. A very high rate of interest is charged if the entire credit card bill is not paid in full by the due date.

People can search online to compare different credit card offers before signing up for one. Many credit cards include

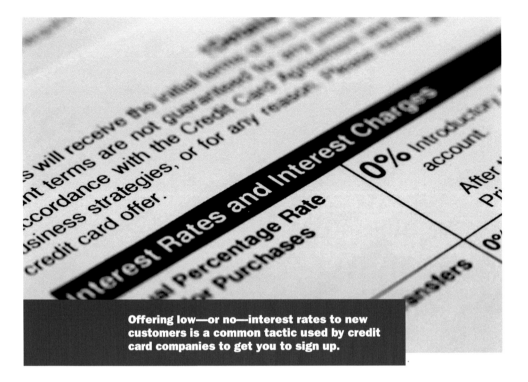

Offering low—or no—interest rates to new customers is a common tactic used by credit card companies to get you to sign up.

conveniences such as the ability to check balances and recent transactions online and download account information into personal finance programs. Consumers can use websites like Bankrate.com, Consumer-action.org, and CardRatings.com to compare credit card services and fees.

Sometimes a special low interest rate is offered when people sign up for a new card. Be aware that the rate may end in a few months and a higher one may go into effect. People get penalties (they are charged extra fees) if they pay their bill late or charge more than their credit limit. Their interest rate may also go up. If possible, try to find a credit card that has no annual fee and a low interest rate on the amount owed.

By using credit cards wisely, young people can establish a good credit history. In turn, this good credit can help them get auto loans, student loans for college, and home loans. There are some good reasons to use credit cards. Buying online and in local stores with a credit card is usually easier and safer than paying by check. Checks include information a thief could use to access an account. Sometimes people pay by credit card for a large, unexpected expense, such as car brakes that suddenly go out. Using credit can help people manage such purchases if their emergency fund is low. People may also charge an item to take advantage of a sale and then pay later.

However, credit cards can make impulse buying and overspending easy. Cardholders need to be careful not to spend more than they can afford to pay back. If just the minimum required payment on a credit card bill is made, most of the money goes to pay interest or finance charges. Not much is left to pay the principal, or the original amount borrowed. People may end up spending much more than the item's original price.

Overcharging can lead to major debt problems and a poor credit report. This situation can limit one's ability to get loans for cars or school or to rent an apartment. Some employers even cancel job opportunities after discovering a candidate has a poor credit record.

A poor credit rating can affect your loan options when you go to make a big purchase like a car.

A Card with a Difference

Both debit cards and credit cards let people spend money without having to carry cash. Using them to buy products is fast and easy. The two types of cards have important differences, though. A debit card is linked to a checking account. When making a purchase with a debit card, money is electronically taken out of the checking account and immediately transferred to the store's account. Banks may charge an annual fee for a debit card or a small fee for each transaction.

With their debit card and a personal identification number, people can electronically withdraw cash from their checking account at an automated teller machine (ATM). Withdrawals occur immediately. Banks may limit how much money can be taken out in a twenty-four-hour period. At ATMs, people can also make deposits or transfer funds between accounts.

Many banks charge a fee every time a debit card is used at another bank's ATM. These fees can add up quickly. Sometimes people use their debit card and accidentally spend or withdraw more than they have in their account. The bank may pay the overage but will charge the customer a hefty penalty.

Be careful to conceal your PIN when you use an ATM in order to protect your funds from thieves.

Stocks, Bonds, and Other Investments

Investments such as stocks, bonds, and mutual funds can help your money to grow. Such investments can be handled in person at branch offices of financial investing companies. Increasingly, these companies have online arms, and some companies are completely operated on the web. Online investing may save money and time by eliminating costs for branch offices. Accepting and processing trades on the internet can be more cost efficient, too. Be sure to compare fees, services, and rates for brokers and major mutual fund companies, whether you opt to visit local establishments or transact your business online. Keep in mind that

(continued on the next page)

Stock prices and values are volatile, or subject to rapid increases and decreases. The stock market is a risky game to play, but it can pay off well.

(continued from the previous page)

inexpensive electronic investment companies may have limited products and services and may be less likely to offer prompt assistance. You may feel more comfortable dealing one on one with brokers while you are learning the investing ropes.

While online trading might save transaction costs, the ease of the experience might encourage you to trade more than you should. This situation could result in higher total costs and lower investment returns. It may also be tempting to shift funds around in order to respond to temporary fluctuations in the stock market. Although this action may seem wise at the time, it could end up hurting you in the long run, since steady growth and long-term investments often make more money than daily wheeling and dealing.

Accounting for Savings

Banks and credit unions pay customers interest for using the money they deposit in their savings accounts. In turn, this interest encourages people to save. These accounts are safe places to hold money that is not needed right away. The federal government insures accounts up to $250,000 at banks and credit unions through the Federal Deposit Insurance Corporation.

Interest rates can vary over a period of time and for different accounts. A bank's website can be used to view account information and transfer funds between accounts. Savings account information can be downloaded to personal finance software and apps, too.

Teens can do research online and compare savings accounts. Most banks have a website where they post savings options and interest rates. Compounding is key to saving because interest can be earned on savings and on the interest the money earns. Teens will want to find out how much interest is paid and when. Interest may be paid daily, monthly, quarterly, or yearly. This rate of occurrence impacts the amount of interest

Reputable banks and credit unions have their accounts insured by the FDIC.

earned. Even 1 or 2 percent interest paid on money in a savings account can make a big difference in the long term. To compare rates at local banks or around the country, the federal government recommends using Bankrate.com.

On the web, teens can find out the minimum amount a bank requires for customers to open a savings account. They will also want to determine how easy it is to put money in and take money out of a bank's savings account. Banks usually charge a fee when a savings account balance falls below a minimum amount. Fees vary from bank to bank.

Keeping Track of Money

Online tools and personal software can help teens stick to a budget or spending plan. Personal finance programs help people see how they spend, save, and invest their money. They can then decide if they need to make changes to meet their spending and saving goals. It does take time to learn how to use these programs and keep them up to date.

Many banking sites allow customers to link to online accounts at other banks, credit unions, credit card companies, and financial institutions. Money can be tracked at any time by computer or smartphone. Most banks provide this service on their website, usually at no charge.

Similar programs are offered by nonbank websites, such as Mint, YNAB, and Yodlee Money Center. These sites provide free tools and advice to help people with budgeting. Some have chat rooms where ideas about money can be shared with other members. When people log in to their accounts on these sites, all of their transactions are pulled together. They can view their spending, pay bills, and transfer funds. They can see how much money goes to buy gas and pay for rent, entertainment, or eating out. Financial information on these sites and online banking sites is password protected and kept safe by security technology.

Another way to track money digitally is to enter spending and other financial information into computer software. Smartphone apps are also available for this purpose. People can track and manage their savings, investments, debts, and loans. They can also use word processing or spreadsheet software to set up a money management system.

One reason teens may want to use money management tools is to make sure they have funds to cover their current purchases and to pay for future college and emergency expenses. To have the appropriate funds, they need to keep accurate records of the dates and amounts of checks and debit card purchases. They can keep copies or access electronic versions of bank account and credit card statements. It is important to save ATM and deposit slips, canceled checks, and any receipts for purchases. Teens also need to make sure they record all transactions in their checkbook register or money management app.

10 Great Questions to Ask a Banker

1. What online services are available to help me learn how to budget money and pay bills?

2. How much time will it take me to plan and set up a budget online or with computer software?

3. How many credit cards and online bank accounts should I have?

4. I scheduled an automatic payment online but then changed my mind. What should I do?

5. How am I protected if someone steals and then uses my credit card or debit card?

6. Should I use my credit card, debit card, or bank account number to prove my identity?

7. Some websites that provide free budgeting tools carry advertising for things online. Can I trust these ads?

8. Should I be investing money online? What are the best online investments for me?

9. Rates for a car loan at a web-only bank and a brick-and-mortar local bank may be different. Why?

10. What information do I need to save from digital and paper account statements?

CHAPTER THREE

Internet Shopping

t's all too easy to overspend online. In order to avoid that, teens should think carefully about what they want to buy so that they don't fall victim to impulse buys. Teens should also set a budget, compare prices, and find vendors they trust.

Buying online has some disadvantages. People cannot do hands-on inspection of products or try on merchandise such as clothes, shoes, or jewelry. They cannot talk face to face with the seller or salesperson. Other issues can arise, including late delivery of items, shipment of wrong or damaged items, and hidden fees. Teens should know the quality expected of the product or service, promised arrival time, warranty, return policy, and if the company provides support for questions or problems.

How Buying Online Works

Although every site is a little different, selecting and paying for an item through a computer or a smartphone is similar. To find a product, people might type keywords in an internet browser

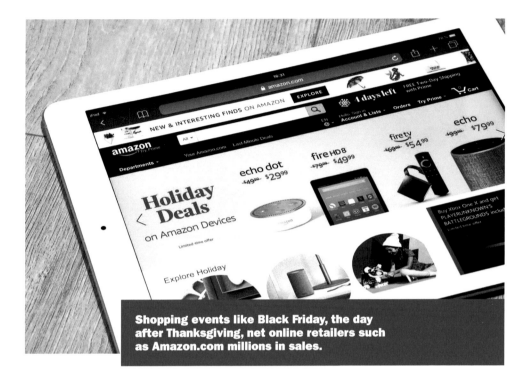

Shopping events like Black Friday, the day after Thanksgiving, net online retailers such as Amazon.com millions in sales.

such as Google Chrome, Safari, Firefox, Bing, or Microsoft Edge. Then they click on the links that display possible websites where they can buy the desired item. Sometimes people go directly to a company's site, such as Amazon.com, to shop. There, they can read information about products, see prices, and read reviews.

When shoppers choose an item, they click on a button such as Buy, Add to Cart, Add to Bag, or Add to Basket. The item is put into an online shopping cart, bag, or basket. Then they can continue shopping or start the checkout process.

At checkout, buyers can review their cart or bag to make sure the items and quantities are correct. Then they complete one or more pages of forms with information such as their name, email address, street address, phone number, and shipping instructions. Entering payment information and any promo or coupon codes

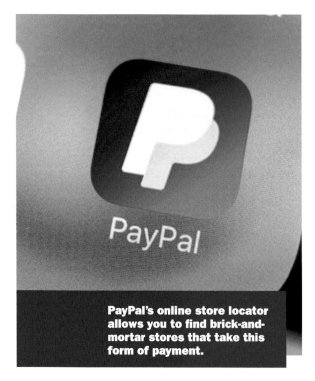

PayPal's online store locator allows you to find brick-and-mortar stores that take this form of payment.

comes next. Buyers usually have options for paying, such as with a credit card or through PayPal. Services like PayPal securely store all payment information for people, including their bank account or credit card numbers. Buyers can then pay or send money without showing their financial information to others.

Once an order is placed, a confirmation page appears with an order or reference number and purchase details. A confirmation is also sent to the email address provided during checkout. Teens should save this information on their computer or smartphone or print it. They may need it if problems with shipping occur or other questions arise.

Getting a Good Deal

One benefit of shopping online is the ability to research a product before buying or deciding not to buy. Doing research can help people determine the best price for an item and if the seller is trustworthy. Shoppers can access various sources for product reviews. Amazon is widely used by people to post and read product reviews. Retailers' sites may have reviews of their

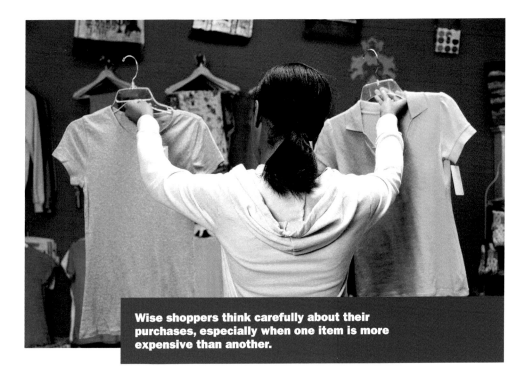

Wise shoppers think carefully about their purchases, especially when one item is more expensive than another.

products or services. Another way to research products is to use sites that offer or collect reviews. With just a click, people can turn to sites such as Review.com and Consumersearch.com to see what others have to say about a product.

Teens might want to go to several sites to shop because no one site has the best deal every time. Some sites, such as Shopping .com and PriceGrabber.com, provide tax and shipping costs along with the product's price. Other comparison sites are BizRate.com, Shopzilla.com, and BeatMyDeal.com. Specialized online shopping directories can be useful for finding electronics, clothing, shoes, or sporting goods all in one place.

Comparison Shopping on the Go

Some smartphone apps combine in-store shopping with online information. In-store shoppers can look up reviews and prices by scanning the barcode of a product with their smartphone. Apps such as PriceCheck.com, Purchx, Scan Life, TTPM, or those put out by Amazon and Walmart provide price and discount comparisons. With some apps, people can speak the product name into their smartphone or snap a photo of a product to find more information. People using ShopSavvy can scan for prices and see if an item is available online or in local stores. Ratings, the *Consumer Reports* app, gives people access to the product reviews, ratings, and comparisons of products and services done by *Consumer Reports*. This independent magazine, published by the Consumers Union, does not accept advertising.

Special Deals and Coupons

Coupon codes can impact final costs when shopping online. People can search for a store along with keywords like "discount," "coupon," "coupon code," "promo code," or "free shipping" to find available discounts.

Social couponing gives people group-purchasing power to get deep discounts on a variety of products and services. Sellers offering group coupons hope to attract new customers to try their products or services. They also hope people will share

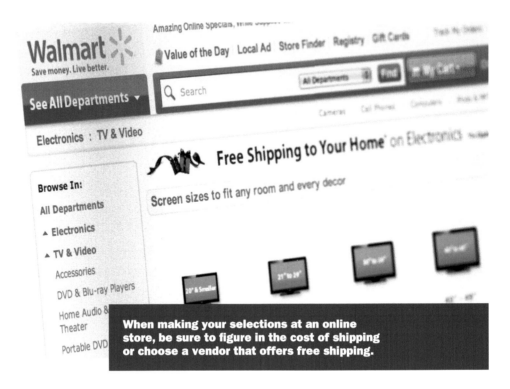

Walmart
Save money. Live better.

Amazing Online Specials,

Value of the Day   Local Ad   Store Finder   Registry   Gift Cards

See All Departments

Search   All Departments

Electronics : TV & Video

Free Shipping to Your Home on Electronics

Browse In:

All Departments

▲ Electronics

  ▲ TV & Video

   Accessories

   DVD & Blu-ray Players

   Home Audio & Theater

   Portable DVD

Screen sizes to fit any room and every decor

When making your selections at an online store, be sure to figure in the cost of shipping or choose a vendor that offers free shipping.

the information with family and friends via email, Facebook, or Twitter. To use social couponing, people sign up at a website and receive coupon or voucher offers every day, which they can print and redeem (use). Deals are usually offered for use during a short period of time, such as one day. Groupon, LivingSocial, and Scoutmob are all sites that provide group deals. Some city news sites also have local group coupons.

Social coupons may offer large discounts on clothing, shoes, household items, cultural events, restaurants, sporting goods, and services for cars and other vehicles. Unlike with regular coupons, consumers must pay for the item (such as a dinner for two) up front in order to take advantage of the deal. Some coupons or vouchers must be used right away, while others have a longer expiration date.

Groupon goods usually have a limited quantity, and when they are gone the deal is over. LivingSocial offers a deal every day with deep discounts at local restaurants, theaters, and more. Scoutmob sends group deals to smartphones.

Giving in to Temptation

It can be tempting to make impulsive purchases when shopping online. People may find it difficult to resist a good deal, particularly if a store highlights a discounted item for a limited time. Sometimes they buy more products or services online than they had budgeted for or spend more than they had planned. Or they may buy something and then forget about it because the items can take days or weeks to arrive.

Small costs can pile up fast. A song or movie may cost a dollar or two, but some people impulsively download hundreds in a short time. People might sign up for online music or movie subscriptions that are automatically charged to their credit card or bank account every month. However, they might not remember they had done so or know how to cancel them. Although one service might cost $10 a month, multiple services add up.

Some people become compulsive shoppers. Compulsive shoppers regularly buy many unnecessary things. The appeal of shopping for these people is the process of searching out and obtaining a new or better item. These shoppers find the process so exciting that the desire to buy overrides their spending plans. This can leave them deep in debt.

Both impulsive and compulsive buyers may experience financial stress when their credit card bills are due. Some may have used debit cards to buy merchandise with money from their bank accounts. As a result, they may not have enough money for necessary items, like gas or car insurance, or to pay their rent and utility (water, heat, and electricity) bills.

Teens can take steps to rein in impulse buying. When shopping, it's important to weigh needs versus wants. After putting an item in an online shopping cart, teens can walk away before ordering it and think about what else their money is needed for. This pause can help them cool off and decide if they really should buy the item. Turning off shopping alerts helps curb impulse buying. Converting monthly costs of automatic subscriptions to an annual cost is one way to see the impact on a budget clearly. Teens who stick to their budgets tend to avoid overspending and acting impulsively or compulsively.

Consumer Rights with Online Shopping

The Federal Trade Commission (FTC) requires online companies to follow rules. Companies must ship an item within the time promised. If no delivery time is stated, they must ship within thirty days of receiving an order. Another rule requires businesses to notify customers if an item cannot be shipped on time. Customers can then choose to wait or cancel the order and get a refund. After canceling, the money must be refunded within seven days or credited within one billing cycle if charged on a credit card.

Once purchases are received, customers have the right to return a defective item and get their money back. Companies also often allow the exchange of clothing, shoes, and other items to get a correct fit. For exchanges of an online purchase, people may have to pay for the return shipping, in addition to the original shipping costs.

Sometimes people receive an item and decide they do not want it. The company's policy determines if store credit or a

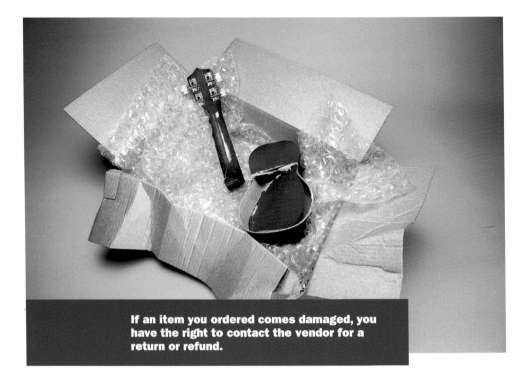

If an item you ordered comes damaged, you have the right to contact the vendor for a return or refund.

refund is issued. Not all stores allow returns. If they do, stores differ in their policies and may charge fees for return shipping or restocking an item. Even if an online store accepts returns, it may issue refunds only by the method of payment or by giving customers credit to buy other items at the store. There may also be a time limit on returns. For example, customers may have only thirty days to return items. For these reasons, shoppers should carefully read the return and cancellation policies on a company's site before buying.

CHAPTER FOUR

Auctions, Ads, and Bartering Online

Once upon a time, people had to place classified ads in newspapers, attend auctions in person, and arrange for trades over the phone. These days, each of these activities can be carried out online. While it is possible to find good deals through these kinds of sites, teens should research what they want to buy beforehand and decide how much to spend.

Particulars of Payment

Teens need to know how to pay for something before buying on a computer or mobile device. Auction sites like eBay and others require members to be at least eighteen years old. A person under eighteen can use an adult's account with the permission of the account holder. However, the account holder is responsible for everything done with that account, including paying for a winning bid.

Sellers choose which type of payment to accept. Some limit buyers to credit cards only. A safe way to use credit cards is to sign up with an online payment service such as PayPal. Some credit card companies also offer this feature. By using an online payment service, buyers never have to show credit or bank information to online businesses or individuals. The seller pays any fees for use of the online payment services.

Some online sellers accept money orders, cashier's checks, personal checks, or cash. Do not use these forms of payment online. Using credit cards provides protections to buyers that money orders and checks do not. People should never send cash through the mail for their purchases. Cash can be easily stolen and is hard to track down if lost.

Building the Biggest Auction Site

Major online auction sites include eBay, uBid, WebStore, and Online Auction. Of these, eBay is the best known. People can find almost anything on eBay, including clothes, household and sporting goods, jewelry, furniture, and even vehicles! People looking for items in a particular category, such as computers, electronics, art, or collectibles, may want to go to sites that auction only those items.

In 1995, Pierre Omidyar opened the website that later became eBay. The first item that sold, a broken laser pointer, was to Canadian Mark Fraser. Omidyar talked his friend Jeff Skoll into becoming the company's president. The following year, the

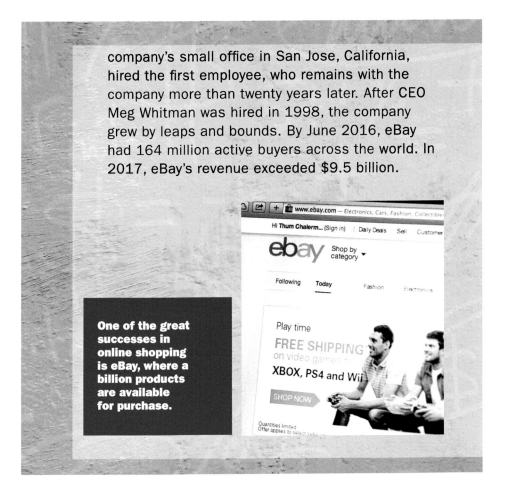

company's small office in San Jose, California, hired the first employee, who remains with the company more than twenty years later. After CEO Meg Whitman was hired in 1998, the company grew by leaps and bounds. By June 2016, eBay had 164 million active buyers across the world. In 2017, eBay's revenue exceeded $9.5 billion.

One of the great successes in online shopping is eBay, where a billion products are available for purchase.

Online Auction Storefronts

Using internet auction sites can be a good way to buy and sell goods or services. These sites are convenient because they can be accessed day or night. Some offer a huge variety of new and used items from around the world. People may find lower prices on items than they would when shopping at online or local stores. Some sites allow sellers to simply sell an item for a given price. In others, an auction is held with a time limit, and the item is sold to the highest bidder when the auction for that item is closing.

Online auction sites often allow sellers to set a reserve price. This reserve price means the seller will not sell the item below that price. The sites indicate that a reserve price exists but do not show the reserve price to bidders. To win the auction, a bidder must meet or exceed the reserve price and be the highest bidder. The seller and highest bidder do not have a sale if the reserve price is not met. Sometimes people use reverse auction sites such as eBridge to enter details of what they want to buy. The reverse auctioneer forwards their request to other sites. A match may or may not be found.

Bidding and Buying

Auction sites vary as to their rules. On most sites, people need to register and choose a username and password. People can use the site's search tool to browse categories and look for a specific

Christie's is a prestigious auction house founded in London in 1766. Today it offers 350 auctions in more than eighty categories.

item. They can also enter keywords into the search tool to find a product or seller.

Once an item is found, bidders should carefully read the information on the page. They need to pay attention to the product's description, the seller's terms and conditions, and the payment and shipping methods. Other important information includes the seller's satisfaction rating and buyer feedback. Smart customers learn about any protections they may have, such as free insurance, guarantees for items not delivered or returned, or recourse if the item is not what the seller claimed. Sellers should be willing to answer any questions about their auction items and terms. It is a good idea for bidders to make electronic or print copies of all transaction information.

Many auction sites have two ways to buy an item—by fixed price or bidding. A fixed-price item is usually marked with the phrase "Buy It Now" or something similar. By clicking the Buy It Now button, the bidding process is bypassed, and the item is placed in the buyer's cart. People can continue to shop or check out.

Clicking Place Bid or a similar button begins the bidding process. Beforehand, people need to determine their budget for the item and make sure they really want it. They should also set a top price and stick to it. Placing a bid is a legal contract (commitment) to purchase an item.

Proxy bids are a common way to make an initial bid and set a maximum one. People's bids are automatically increased against competing bids until they win the auction or someone outbids their maximum.

After the auction closes, the highest bidder is the winner and is responsible for promptly paying the seller. If the winners do not pay, they have violated their contract and can be kicked off the auction site forever.

Each auction site has its own rules for cancelling a bid during an auction. Most provide a form for bidders to cancel and correct their bid price. Sometimes the item description is changed and bidders no longer want it. People should think carefully about canceling a bid because this information appears on their feedback numbers. This situation can cause sellers to block them from future bidding.

Classified Ads, Internet Style

Using online classified ads is another way to buy products and services. When buyers see an item they want, they contact the site, which uses email to put them in contact with the sellers. Buyers and sellers can exchange emails or agree to meet. Large classified-ad sites include Craigslist.org and Kijiji.ca. They offer the convenience of shopping day or night, and sellers can keep the ads up to date. These general sites offer free ads, except for some real estate and job ads. Other smaller classified-ad sites focus on specific items, such as books, clothes, computers and electronics, cars, antiques, or collectibles.

Most online ads are posted on Craigslist, which has sites for cities small and large all over the world. The ads on Craigslist are local. This aspect means the buyer and seller can choose to meet in person to complete the deal. In this case, the buyer does not pay for shipping, and the seller may not need an online payment service. However, teens should exchange goods in this way only with the help and supervision of an adult. If the item is costly, both the seller and buyer may want to sign an agreement about their transaction.

Before buying anything on a classified site, people will want to read the site's terms and conditions and any safety tips, and

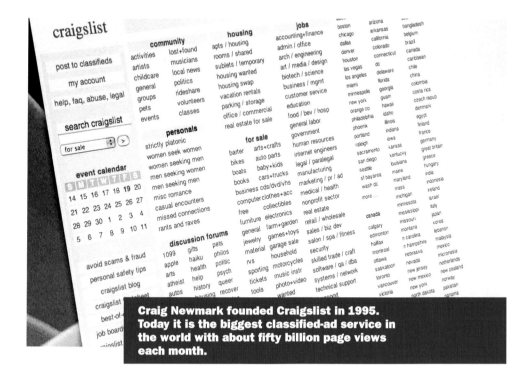

Craig Newmark founded Craigslist in 1995. Today it is the biggest classified-ad service in the world with about fifty billion page views each month.

they should understand how to report abuse. Buyers should never include a personal phone number when responding to an ad. It is best to deal with local people and meet face to face at a public place like a coffee shop, fast-food restaurant, or local library. Teens should bring a parent or other trusted adult to the meeting. Buyers should carefully check over the item before paying for it. If the item is a computer or other electronic item, plug it in or try it out to make sure it works.

Local Facebook garage sale groups and buy/sell/trade groups are becoming increasingly popular places to post items for sale. Facebook's Marketplace option also shows products for sale in local areas.

While in-person flea markets still exist, much of people's buying, selling, and trading of goods has moved online to Facebook and other digital marketplaces.

Trading Online

People use online swapping to trade goods or services like snow shoveling, lawn mowing, or dog walking in exchange for things they want. They may be able to get lightly used items for free or just for the cost of shipping. There are a variety of swaps, reuse directories, and materials exchange sites. Some sites offer free exchanges or bulletin boards. Others charge a user fee.

Popular trading sites include TradeAway.com and BarterOnly.com. PaperbackSwap.com has a service in which people exchange paperback books, hardbacks, textbooks, and audiobooks. TitleTrader .com offers similar services. Swapright.com allows people to exchange services such as child care, home improvement, and health and beauty services.

Myths and Facts

Myth It is best to make buying decisions based solely on online customer reviews.

Fact Customer reviews are only opinions and may provide useful insight into the contents of items or how they work. Although they can help as purchasing guides, people should make buying decisions based on their budget, needs, wants, personal taste, and quality of the product.

Myth An online auction bid can be cancelled if a better price is found at another online auction.

Fact Finding the same item for a lower price does not count as a reason to cancel a bid.

Myth People can get their money back for digital gift cards that they lose.

Fact Some financial institutions and companies issue prepaid electronic gift cards, telephone cards, and mass transit passes. Most digital gift cards are not covered if lost or misused.

Myth Almost all retail shopping occurs in online stores.

Fact While young people are more comfortable shopping online, as of 2017 only around 10 percent of purchases are made online. Still, this number is increasing from year to year.

CHAPTER FIVE

Keeping Your Money Safe

While the internet gives people the opportunity to buy almost anything one can think of, this convenience comes with dangers. Online scams exist. Many—if not most—internet stores collect and sell information about who buys what, where, and how. Teens can protect themselves from scams and privacy leaks by using certain practices while shopping and doing business.

Spam and Scams

One of the best guidelines to follow when shopping online is to know the seller. People can research a seller by going to the business's website and looking for a section called About Us. State and local consumer offices may have information about a company. Some online sellers are members of programs such as the Better Business Bureau (BBB). Companies that carry the BBB

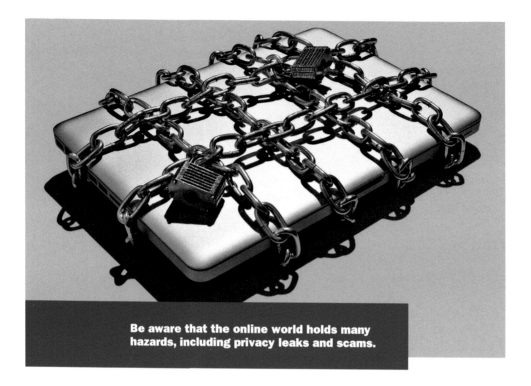

Be aware that the online world holds many hazards, including privacy leaks and scams.

Accredited Business seal for the web have been checked out by the BBB. However, this seal is not a guarantee of a seller's good business practices. The BBB site provides ratings (with letter grades A, B, C, D, or F) to show if a company is reliable and willing to resolve customers' concerns.

Another way to find out about online sellers is to search for consumers' comments. Using a search engine, enter a company's name and a term such as "review," "rating," "scam," or "complaint." Teens can also read buyers' ratings of online stores at Bizrate.com. Some auction sites, such as eBay, post ratings of sellers based on buyer comments.

An offer that seems too good to be true is probably a scam. Perhaps the seller came by the items illegally or the item is damaged but is not advertised as such. If something goes

Cool necklace, thank you

Mens/boys skull/pirate g

Goods arrived quickly, m

Nail Through Finger. An i

Fab item. Fast Delivery.

Pretty bag/mobile phone

Lovely item. Fast Delivery

Tinkerbelle Fairy Bag No

Online product reviews help shoppers judge whether the product they are considering is worth the cost.

wrong with an online purchase, people should find out whom to contact. They may need to talk to their bank or credit card company or an authority such as the FTC. Federal law protects credit card holders if disputes with a seller come up or if fraudulent (false) charges are made on the card.

Spam email may contain phony offers for products or investments that could end up costing time and money. Many spam messages include a link to unsubscribe from their email lists. People should not click on any links or reply to messages in a spam email. If they do, they could be put on other spam lists. Most email programs have built-in spam filters. A separate program that filters spam and moves suspicious email to a spam or junk

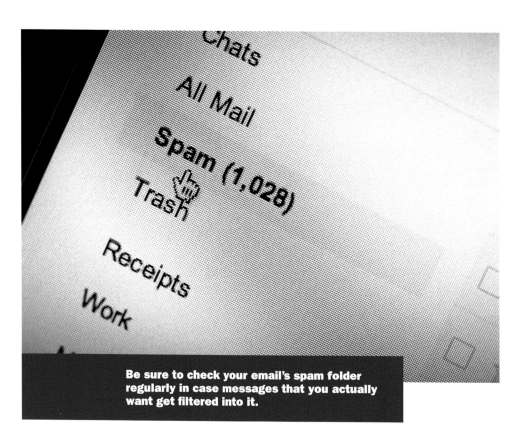

Be sure to check your email's spam folder regularly in case messages that you actually want get filtered into it.

folder can also be installed. Reporting spam can help an email provider track and reduce spam for everyone.

Understanding Privacy in the Online World

The internet is a convenient place to purchase things, transfer money, pay bills, renew driver's licenses, and do other business. However, personal information can be stolen online. To help

Staying Clear of Phishers

Phishing is a fast-growing internet crime. It is the use of email to steal important personal information, such as credit card numbers, passwords, PINs, Social Security numbers, and driver's license numbers. Thieves may use the information to steal a person's identity or empty a bank account. Although these emails are phony, they often seem real. They may claim to come from a bank, credit card, eBay, or other online account. The email says the account has problems and instructs the receiver to click on a link to verify his or her personal information. Never click on these links. Legitimate companies do not ask for passwords, account numbers, or other such personal information by email. Instead, teens should contact the business directly by typing the company's web address into a browser and finding the Contact Us or similar section.

protect privacy, people can look for and read privacy statements on websites. It's important to make sure companies do not sell details about customers to other companies. Policy statements are usually found on companies' websites in the About or FAQ section. The policies explain how information is collected and protected.

People will want to stick with secure web pages when doing online transactions. These sites encrypt (scramble) personal information to make it difficult to change or steal. One signal of security is an unbroken key or a closed lock to the left of the internet address or on the bottom of a web page. Another signal of a secure site is that the first letters of the internet address are "https." If a site is secure, the likelihood of identity theft is usually low.

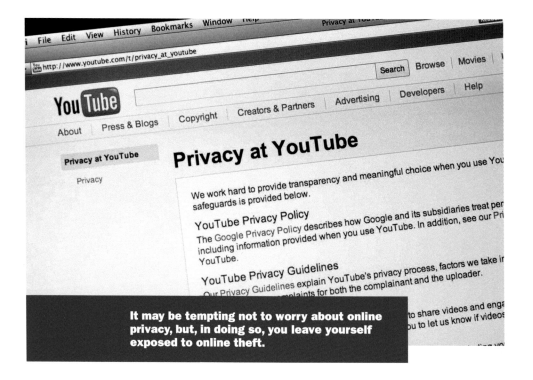

It may be tempting not to worry about online privacy, but, in doing so, you leave yourself exposed to online theft.

Spyware is often put onto computers and smartphones as people browse the internet. These programs track what people do when they are online. Tracking can help companies figure out how to use advertising to sell things to consumers. For example, if someone searches for "movie reviews," an ad might pop up for a new movie coming to theaters soon. Sometimes spyware is used to steal passwords and other personal information. To help with this problem, an antispyware program can be installed and run regularly.

Adware can include spyware. Even if it doesn't, it displays ads to certain products. Often, adware is installed in free software.

Keeping Your Identity

Identity theft is when someone steals and illegally uses a person's name, credit card number, Social Security number, or other personal information. Thieves might use the information to sign up for cell phone services and run up large bills, open credit card accounts and buy many costly items, or take out a loan. The National Crime Prevention Council estimates that identity theft happens to millions of people every year, and about one-third of the victims are between eighteen and twenty-nine years old. Teens are at high risk because they frequently use the internet and share personal information on blogs and social networking sites such as Facebook and Snapchat.

People need to be careful about identity theft because they are responsible for any debts in their name. They may have trouble getting credit cards and, in some states, even driver's licenses due to bad credit histories. Many hours of hard work—and sometimes thousands of dollars in legal fees—may be needed to restore a damaged credit history.

Buying and using a shredder for your sensitive information can help protect it from thieves.

Reduce the risk of identity theft by tearing up or shredding credit card offers, account statements, unwanted receipts, and other financial documents before throwing them away. At ATMs, people should use their free hand to block others from seeing the keyboard when entering their PIN. When using a computer or smartphone, teens should be careful to keep others from seeing their personal information.

Teens should not tell their passwords or PINs to anyone, not even a friend. It is smart to avoid family or pet names, common words, telephone numbers, birthdays, and other information that may be easy to guess when creating passwords. Someone who guesses a password may be able to log in to accounts or pose online as that teen. The longer the password, the tougher it is to crack. For PINs, an address, telephone number, Social Security number, or birth date should not be used. A password or PIN should be changed if one suspects that someone else knows it.

Report identity theft immediately. Call the financial institution at the phone number on the account statement or on the back of the credit or debit card. Any accounts the thief used should be closed. Next, report the fraud to the local police and keep a copy of the police report in a safe place. Victims can file a report with the Federal Trade Commission as well. They can also place a fraud alert with one of the three credit reporting bureaus: Equifax, Experian, or TransUnion.

Taking Responsibility

Many people use the internet to shop and handle financial matters. Every time customers are asked to provide personal information—whether in an online form, email, text, or phone message—they need to decide if they can really trust the request. Each person must protect his or her money.

People want to be careful about storing and displaying personal information online. For example, they should not store their credit card information on websites and apps. When using smartphones, people can limit the amount of personal information stored in the device. They can also use the "lock" function so that others cannot access their smartphone. When a computer is not in use, lock it. People should avoid doing financial transactions on public Wi-Fi, offered in some libraries, stores, coffee shops, and other places because personal information is not protected. Teens can limit who can access their social networking profiles and create different lists of people who can view their posted information.

When using ATMs, people need to be alert to their surroundings and prevent others from seeing their PIN. Memorize PINs; do not write them down. People should avoid carrying their PIN or Social Security number in a wallet, purse, or backpack.

An important money protection step is to monitor banking and credit card accounts regularly. This scrutiny can help teens find unusual purchases or activities, which they should check out right away. Also, teens need to compare the bank's records to their own records to make sure they agree. If there is a problem, they should contact the bank as soon as possible.

Following these guidelines will help teens manage their money online and keep their personal information safe. This strategy will allow them to enjoy the convenience of shopping, budgeting, and managing their money online now and in the future.

GLOSSARY

automated teller machine (ATM) An electronic machine that performs basic banking functions, such as withdrawals and deposits.

budget A plan for how to use one's money.

chat room A virtual room where people have online interactive discussions.

checking account A bank account that allows a person to take out money, pay bills, or buy things by writing checks or making withdrawals.

comparison shopping The practice of researching products and services to buy the highest quality at the lowest price.

compound interest Interest that is earned on an amount of money (usually savings), as well as on the accumulated interest on that money.

cosigner Someone who acts as a joint signer, guaranteeing payment if the primary signer does not make payments.

credit An agreement in which someone buys something now and promises to pay for it later.

credit card A plastic card issued by banks, stores, and other businesses that allows the cardholder to buy products and services on credit. Credit cards charge interest, usually beginning one month after a purchase is made.

credit history A record of an individual's past borrowing and repaying.

debit card A plastic card used to withdraw money directly from a checking account or to make payments electronically without having to write a check.

debt An amount of money owed to another party, usually after having borrowed it.

emergency fund An amount of money set aside to be used in an emergency, such as the loss of a job, an illness, or another large, unexpected expense.

fraud The crime of using deception for personal financial gain.

identity theft The theft and use of a name, Social Security number, credit card number, or other personal information for illegal purposes.

interest A charge paid for the use of borrowed money.

investing The act of committing money to an asset, such as stock, property, etc., in order to make a profit in the future.

loan A sum of money borrowed for a certain amount of time.

overage An amount by which a transaction (such as a withdrawal or a payment) is too much.

overdraft fee A penalty payment for having a negative balance in an account.

recourse An opportunity to use or do something in order to deal with a problem.

savings account A bank account in which money is deposited for safekeeping and earning interest at a modest rate.

spreadsheet program A computer program that arranges information, often financial data, in a table, chart, or graph.

statement A summary of account activity issued by banks, credit card companies, or other financial institutions.

transaction A transfer of money from one account, person, party, etc., to another. Withdrawals and deposits are typical transactions at banks and other financial institutions.

Wi-Fi A wireless networking technology that uses radio waves to provide a wireless high-speed internet connection.

FOR MORE INFORMATION

Canadian Bankers Association (CBA)
Box 348
Commerce Court West
199 Bay Street, 30th Floor
Toronto, ON M5L 1G2
Canada
(800) 263-0231
Email: inform@cba.ca
Website: http://www.cba.ca
Twitter: @CdnBankers
The Canadian Bankers Association provides information
about money, budgeting, credit, investments, and
banking in Canada.

Consumer Federation of America (CFA)
1620 I Street NW, Suite 200
Washington, DC 20006
(202) 387-6121
Email: cfa@consumerfed.org
Website: http://www.consumerfed.org
Facebook: @ConsumerFederationofAmerica
Twitter: @ConsumerFed
The Consumer Federation of America is an advocacy,
research, and education organization providing
information on personal finances, including money
management and budgeting.

Federal Deposit Insurance Corporation (FDIC)
550 17th Street NW
Washington, DC 20429-9990
(877) ASK-FDIC [275-3342]
Website: http://www.fdic.gov
Facebook and Twitter: @FDICgov
The FDIC protects individuals against the loss of deposits.
    This agency also provides information on shopping
    for financial services, understanding consumer
    rights, and avoiding financial fraud.

Federal Trade Commission (FTC)
600 Pennsylvania Avenue NW
Washington, DC 20580
(202) 326-2222
Website: http://www.ftc.gov
Facebook: @federaltradecommission
Twitter: @FTC
The Federal Trade Commission works to prevent
    fraudulent, misleading, and unfair business practices
    in the marketplace and to provide information to help
    people spot, stop, and avoid them.

Financial Literacy and Education Commission
Office of Financial Education Department of the Treasury
1500 Pennsylvania Avenue NW
Washington, DC 20220
(800) FED-INFO [333-4636]
Website: http://www.mymoney.gov
The Financial Literacy and Education Commission offers
    information from various federal agencies on money
    management and budgeting.

Financial Planning Standards Council (FPSC)
902–375 University Avenue
Toronto, ON M5G 2J5
Canada
(800) 305-9886
Email: inform@fpsc.ca
Website: http://www.fpsc.ca
Facebook: @FPSC.Canada
Twitter: @FPSC_Canada
The Financial Planning Standards Council provides
    information for teens on personal finance, budgeting,
    savings, investments, and more.

Institute of Consumer Financial Education (ICFE)
PO Box 34070
San Diego, CA 92163
(619) 239-1401
Website: http://www.financial-education-icfe.org
The Institute of Consumer Financial Education is
    a nonprofit public education organization that
    promotes wise credit use, saving, and investing.

Jump$tart Coalition for Personal Financial Literacy
1001 Connecticut Avenue NW, Suite 640
Washington, DC 20036
(202) 846-6780
Email: info@jumpstart.org
Website: http://www.jumpstart.org
Facebook and Twitter: @natljumpstart
Jump$tart offers information on money management,
    budgeting, credit, investing, and savings. Go to its
    clearinghouse to find a list of books and other print
    materials, CDs, DVDs, videos, and websites.

FOR FURTHER READING

Bickerstaff, Linda. *Smart Strategies for Saving and Building Wealth.* New York, NY: Rosen Publishing, 2015.

Blohm, Craig E. *Teen Guide to Credit and Debt.* San Diego, CA: ReferencePoint Press, Inc., 2017.

Hardyman, Robyn. *Understanding Buying and Spending.* New York, NY: Rosen Publishing, 2018.

Hardyman, Robyn. *Understanding Credit and Debt.* New York, NY: Rosen Publishing, 2018.

Marsico, Katie. *Using Credit Wisely.* Ann Arbor, MI: Cherry Lake Publishing, 2016.

McGuire, Kara. *Making Money Work: The Teens' Guide to Saving, Investing, and Building Wealth.* North Mankato, MN: Capstone Young Readers, 2015.

McGuire, Kara. *The Teen Money Manual: A Guide to Cash, Credit, Spending, Saving, Work, Wealth, and More.* North Mankato, MN: Capstone Young Readers, 2015.

Minden, Cecelia. *Living on a Budget.* Ann Arbor, MI: Cherry Lake Publishing, 2016.

Nagle, Jeanne. *Money, Banking, and Finance.* New York, NY: Rosen Publishing, 2018.

Peterson, Judy Monroe. *Smart Strategies for Investing Wisely and Successfully.* New York, NY: Rosen Publishing, 2015.

Schlesinger, Emily, and Jennifer Liss. *Managing Money.* Costa Mesa, CA: Saddleback Educational Publishing, 2017.

Weeks, Marcus, and Derek Braddon. *Heads Up Money.* New York, NY: DK Publishing, 2016.

BIBLIOGRAPHY

Benson, April Lane. "Don't Shop, Swap! Redux."
    Psychology Today, May 31, 2011. http://www
    .psychologytoday.com/blog/buy-or-not-buy
    /201105/dont-shop-swap-redux.

Bickle, Marianne. "The Economic Benefit of Rising Gas
    Prices." *Forbes*, February 21, 2012. https://www
    .forbes.com/sites/prospernow/2012/02/21
    /the-economic-benefit-of-rising-gas-prices
    /#24fcdc785315.

Duffy, Jill. "The Best Personal Finance Services of 2018."
    PCMAG, August 27, 2018. http://www.pcmag.com
    /article2/0,2817,2407617,00.asp.

eBay. "Our History." Retrieved October 3, 2018. http://
    www.ebayinc.com/our-company/our-history.

Federal Trade Commission. "Electronic Banking." August
    2012. https://www.consumer.ftc.gov/articles/0218
    -electronic-banking.

Fiegerman, Seth. "Impulse Buys: The Real Risk of Online
    Shopping." MainStreet.com, February 9, 2011.
    https://www.thestreet.com/story/12787637/1
    /impulse-buys-real-risk-online-shopping.html.

Gordon, Rachel Singer. *Point, Click, and Save: Mashup
    Mom's Guide to Saving and Making Money Online*.
    Medford, NJ: CyberAge Books, 2010.

Karp, Gregory. *The 1-2-3 Money Plan: The Three Most
    Important Steps to Saving and Spending Smart*.
    Upper Saddle River, NJ: FT Press, 2009.

Lynn, Jacquelyn. *Online Shopper's Survival Guide: Order Anything, Anywhere, Anytime*. Irvine, CA: Entrepreneur Press, 2006.

OnGuardOnline.gov. "Computer Security." June 2017. https://www.consumer.ftc.gov/articles/0009-computer-security.

Schwahn, Lauren. "How to Choose the Best Personal Finance Software." NerdWallet, August 22, 2018. http://www.nerdwallet.com/blog/finance/the-best-personal-finance-software-of-2017.

Shinder, Deb. "Money Matters on Your Smartphone." TechRepublic.com, December 19, 2011. https://www.techrepublic.com/blog/smartphones/money-matters-on-your-smartphone/?tag=rbxccnbtr1.

Statista. "EBay's Annual Net Revenue from 2013 to 2017 (in Million US Dollars)." Retrieved October 3, 2018. https://www.statista.com/statistics/507881/ebays-annual-net-revenue.

Steele, Chandra. "The Best Shopping Apps to Compare Prices." *PCMag*, December 3, 2017. http://www.pcmag.com/feature/290959/the-best-shopping-apps-to-compare-prices/5.

Tyson, Eric. P*ersonal Finance for Dummies.* 6th ed. Indianapolis, IN: Wiley Publishing, 2010.

US Department of Justice. "What Are Identity Theft and Identity Fraud?" February 7, 2017. http://www.justice.gov/criminal/fraud/websites/idtheft.html.

INDEX

ABOUT THE AUTHORS

Xina M. Uhl has authored a variety of books for young people in addition to textbooks, teacher's guides, lessons, and assessment questions. When she is not writing or reading, she enjoys travel, photography, and hiking with her dogs. Her blog features her travel adventures and latest fiction projects.

Judy Monroe Peterson holds two master's degrees and is the author of numerous educational books for young people. She is a former technical, health care, and academic librarian and college faculty member; a research scientist; and curriculum editor with more than twenty-five years of experience. She has taught courses at 3M, the University of Minnesota, and Lake Superior College. Currently, she is a writer and editor of K–12 and post-high school curriculum materials on a variety of subjects, including life skills.

PHOTO CREDITS

Cover, p. 1 Vasin Lee/Shutterstock.com; cover, p. 1 (wallet logo) logomills/Shutterstock.com; p. 5 Odua Images/Shutterstock.com; p. 8 Hero Images/Getty Images; p. 9 Trong Nguyen/Shutterstock .com; p. 10 Denys Prykhodov/Shutterstock.com; p. 11 PC Plus Magazine/Future/Getty Images; p. 14 SpeedKingz/Shutterstock.com; p. 16 ImagineerInc/Shutterstock.com; p 17 Casper1774 Studio /Shutterstock.com; p. 18 XiXinXing/Shutterstock.com; p. 19 Mario Tama/Getty Images; p. 21 Patti McConville/Alamy Stock Photo; p. 25 Fotocute/Shutterstock.com; p. 26 BigTunaOnline/Shutterstock .com; p. 27 Paul Simcock/Stockbyte/Getty Images; p. 29 Bloomberg /Getty Images; p. 32 George Diebold/Photographer's Choice/Getty Images; p. 35 aradaphotography/Shutterstock.com; p. 36 Eduardo Munoz Alvarez/Getty Images; p. 39 Vicki Beaver/Alamy Stock Photo; pp. 40–41 Cultura RM Exclusive/Frank and Helena/Getty Images; p. 44 Tim Robberts/Stone/Getty Images; p. 45 incamerastock /Alamy Stock Photo; p. 46 Dejan Stanisavljevic/Shutterstock.com; p. 48 NetPhotos/Alamy Stock Photo; p. 50 NotarYES/Shutterstock.com.

Design: Raúl Rodriguez, R studio T, NYC;
Layout: Tahara Anderson; Photo Researcher: Sherri Jackson